D1200698

TURTLES

by Patrick Merrick

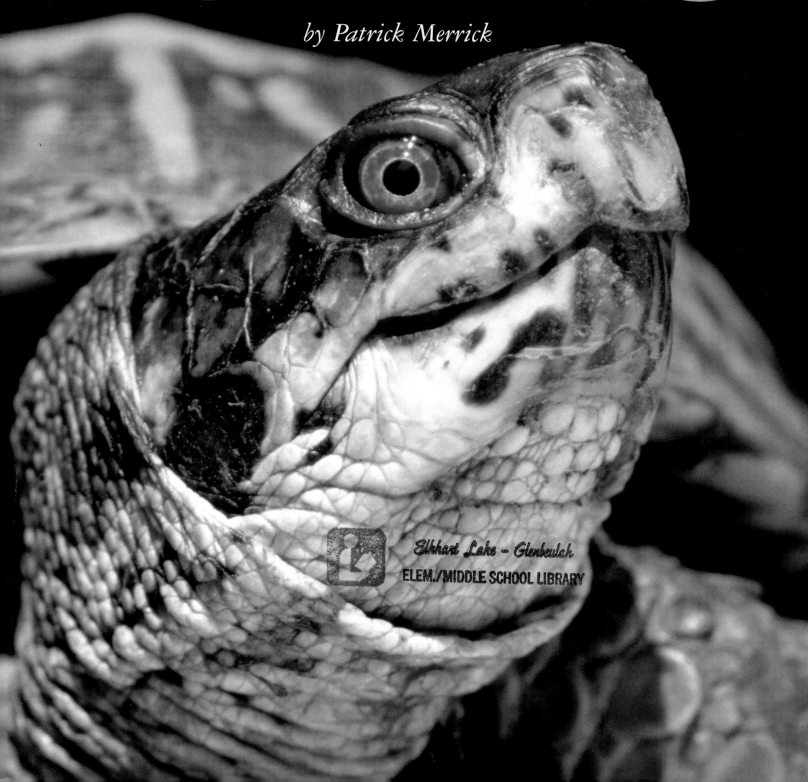

The Child's World

Content Adviser:
Winston Card,
Conservation Program
Manager, Cincinnati Zoo
& Botanical Garden.

Published in the United States of America by The Child's World®
PO Box 326 • Chanhassen, MN 55317-0326
800-599-READ • www.childsworld.com

PHOTO CREDITS
© Darrell Gulin/Corbis: 14–15
© David A. Northcott/Corbis: 17
© E. R. Degginger/Photo Researchers, Inc.: 19
© Herb Segars/Animals Animals–Earth Scenes: 10–11
© iStockphoto.com/Christopher Pattberg: 3
© Joe McDonald/Corbis: 7, 9
© Kevin Schafer/Corbis: 28
© Lynda Richardson/Corbis: 20–21
© Mary Ann McDonald/Corbis: cover, 1
© M. Timothy O'Keefe/Alamy: 24
© Patrick Bennett/Corbis: 25
© Peter Arnold, Inc./Alamy: 27
© Ron Buskirk/Alamy: 5
© S. E. Cornelius/Photo Researchers, Inc.: 22–23
© Stan Osolinski/Dembinsky Photo Associates: 12
© Tim Davis/Corbis: 8

ACKNOWLEDGMENTS
The Child's World®: Mary Berendes, Publishing Director;
Katherine Stevenson, Editor

The Design Lab: Kathleen Petelinsek, Design and Page Production

LIBRARY OF CONGRESS CATALOGING-IN-PUBLICATION DATA
Merrick, Patrick.
 Turtles / by Patrick Merrick.
 p. cm. — (New naturebooks)
 Includes bibliographical references and index.
 ISBN 1-59296-653-5 (library bound : alk. paper)
 1. Turtles—Juvenile literature. I. Title. II. Series.
 QL666.C5M48 2006
 597.92—dc22   2006001380

Table of Contents

On the cover: Eastern box turtles (like the one shown on the cover) are common all across the United States. Males usually have red eyes, while females' eyes are yellow or brown.

Meet the Turtle!

In many places around the world, turtles represent wisdom and long life.

It's a sunny summer day, and you're walking along the edge of a pond. Birds are chirping, and dragonflies and other bugs are zipping through the air. Out in the water, you see several bumps that look like rocks lying on an old log. As you walk a little closer, the "rocks" all slip into the water with a PLOP and disappear! Shortly afterward, a little head pokes back up above the surface, watching you closely. What is this careful creature? It's a turtle!

Here you can see five yellow-bellied sliders basking on a log in Okefenokee Swamp. These turtles get their name from the bright yellow color of their bottom shell. Yellow-bellied sliders are common in the southeastern U.S.

What Are Turtles?

Cold-blooded animals need outside heat to warm their bodies. Turtles and other reptiles often lie in the sun to warm themselves.

Unlike today's turtles, ancient turtles had teeth, and they weren't able to pull their heads into their shells.

Turtles are one form of **reptile**. Reptiles are **cold-blooded** animals that have backbones, lungs for breathing, and scales covering their bodies. Turtles also have a leathery or bony shell, and jaws with no teeth. Many turtles can pull their heads, legs, and tails into their shells for protection.

Turtles have been around for a long time. In fact, the earliest turtles lived at about the same time as the first dinosaurs, over 200 million years ago! Today there are over 250 different types, or **species**, of turtles. The smallest types are only about 4 inches (10 cm) long and weigh less than 4 ounces (113 g). The largest are leatherback sea turtles, which can be over 8 feet (2 m) long and weigh 1,800 pounds (816 kg)!

Red-eared sliders like this one get their name from the red stripes on the sides of their heads. These pond turtles are found in many parts of the U.S. and grow to be about 8 inches (20 cm) long.

Are Turtles and Tortoises Different?

Turtles and tortoises can live for a long time. Smaller species often reach 30 years. Snapping turtles can live to be 60 or more, and American box turtles can live to be 100. One Madagascar radiated tortoise lived for 188 years, and one Aldabra giant tortoise might have lived to 250!

Scientists think of turtles and tortoises as one type of animal—reptiles with shells. They divide this type into two groups—those that pull their heads straight back into their shells, and those that tuck them to one side.

In North America, however, most people think of these animals in terms of where they live. Those that live in or near water are called "turtles." Those that live on land are called "tortoises." This book talks mostly about turtles.

Turtles are excellent swimmers. Their lighter, flatter shells glide easily through the water, and their webbed feet work like swim fins. Tortoises are better adapted to life on land. Most of them can't swim, and if they get into deep water, they can drown. Their harder, higher shells help protect them from enemies. Their thick feet and legs support their weight as they walk slowly from place to place.

On this page you can see a Galápagos tortoise, while the facing page shows an eastern painted turtle. Can you see how their body shapes are different?

Where Do Turtles Live?

People often think of turtles as slow, but one leatherback was seen swimming at 22 miles (35 km) per hour!

Turtles live all over the world. They live on every **continent** except Antarctica, and throughout most of the world's oceans. They are more common in warmer regions.

There are seven or possibly eight species of turtles that live in the sea. Sea turtles spend almost their entire lives in the water. They are so well adapted to ocean life that their legs look like flippers. They usually stay in shallower water near land. Sometimes they travel into the open ocean.

The only turtle that spends its life in the open ocean is the leatherback turtle. Leatherbacks hold heat better than other turtles, thanks in part to their big bodies and a layer of fat. Leatherbacks can survive even in the cold waters near the Arctic. In fact, they live farther north than any other reptile in the world!

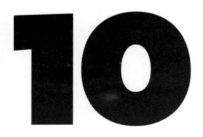

This huge leatherback was swimming off the coast of North Carolina. The photographer noticed that it had some fishing line caught on its back. A team of scientists was able to untangle the line without harming the turtle, and the giant was soon on its way back out to sea.

Many more turtle species live in and around freshwater ponds, lakes, rivers, and marshes. Different types spend different amounts of time in the water or on land.

Even though turtles are more common in warmer regions, they also live in places with cold winters, such as the United States and Canada. What do these turtles do when the weather gets too cold? They **hibernate**, or go into a deep sleep, until it gets warm again. The turtle digs a hole in the ground or deep in the mud at the bottom of a pond. Its heart slows down until it is barely beating. When the turtle is hibernating, it doesn't need to eat or even breathe through its lungs for months at a time!

Some turtles can take in oxygen through their skin and special linings in their mouths and throats. When these turtles are inactive or hibernating, they can go for days or months without coming up for air. Active turtles need to come up for air more often.

This red-eared slider is swimming in a pond on a sunny day. You can see how it uses its front legs to pull itself through the water.

What Do Turtles Look Like?

The leatherback's shell is bendable enough that these turtles can dive more than 3,000 feet (914 m) deep. A hard shell would break with so much water pushing down on it.

Because sea turtles spend so much time in the salty ocean, they build up a lot of salt in their bodies. To get rid of the extra, they shed large, salty tears.

Turtles are easy to recognize because of their shells. A turtle's shell is attached to its skeleton and can never come off. The inner layer of the shell is made up of about 60 flat bones. The bones are covered with thin plates called *scutes*. Scutes are made of the same material as snakes' scales and birds' beaks. The scutes help hold the shell together and make it stronger. Some turtles that spend lots of time in the water, such as leatherbacks and spiny softshells, don't have hard shells. Their shells are soft and leathery instead.

Turtles come in colors that help them blend in with their surroundings, such as olive green, brown, and black. Many of them have patterns on their shells or skin.

14

A turtle's top shell is called a carapace *(KAYR-uh-payss), and the bottom shell is the* plastron *(PLAST-run). They are joined together by bridges. Turtles can feel pain and pressure through their shells.*

What Do Turtles Eat?

Some turtles, such as the American map turtle, eat shelled animals such as snails and clams. Bony ridges on the roofs of their mouths help crush the shells.

The alligator snapping turtle has a wriggly part on its tongue that looks like a worm. Fish that want to eat this "worm" often get eaten by the turtle instead!

Some turtles eat only plants, and others eat only animals. Most turtles, however, are **omnivores** that eat both plants and animals. Most sea turtles eat small animals such as crabs, shellfish, sponges, small fish, or jellyfish, but some eat underwater plants. Loggerheads and ridleys have jaws that can crush and grind shells. Leatherbacks, on the other hand, eat soft foods such as jellyfish. Harder foods would damage their jaws.

Freshwater turtles eat bugs, minnows, fish eggs, worms, snails, tadpoles, mussels, plants that grow in the water, and sometimes dead animals. Snapping turtles are fierce hunters that will eat snakes, rodents, or other turtles. They even sneak up on ducks and other birds and eat them!

Although turtles don't have teeth, their jaws are pointed and have sharp edges, like the beaks of birds. They use their jaws to bite and tear off pieces of food.

Here you can see a western box turtle as it eats an earthworm. These turtles also eat berries, leaves, and fruits, but they especially love to eat beetles.

How Are Baby Turtles Born?

For many types of turtles, how warm the eggs are determines whether they turn into males or females. If the eggs are warmer, they produce mostly females. If they are colder, they produce mostly males.

No matter where turtles spend their lives, they all lay their eggs on land. After mating, the female tries to find a safe place to lay her eggs. Usually she looks for a place in soft sand or dirt, where the eggs will stay warm and moist. Once she finds a good spot, she digs a hole with her back legs and lays her eggs, which are round or oval. Smaller species lay only a few eggs at a time, but larger turtles might lay dozens or over a hundred. When the female is done laying her eggs, she covers up the nest and leaves. The eggs usually hatch about two or three months later. After they hatch, the baby turtles are on their own!

Eastern box turtles like this one usually lay about eight eggs in the early summer. Their eggs take around three months to hatch.

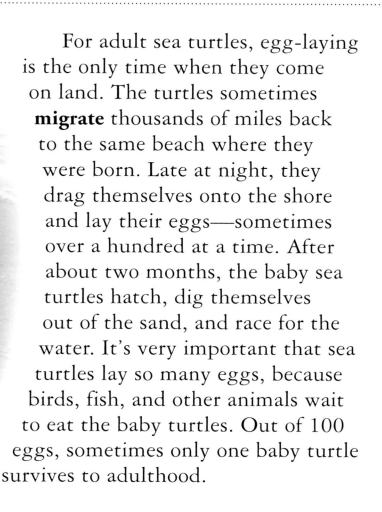

For adult sea turtles, egg-laying is the only time when they come on land. The turtles sometimes **migrate** thousands of miles back to the same beach where they were born. Late at night, they drag themselves onto the shore and lay their eggs—sometimes over a hundred at a time. After about two months, the baby sea turtles hatch, dig themselves out of the sand, and race for the water. It's very important that sea turtles lay so many eggs, because birds, fish, and other animals wait to eat the baby turtles. Out of 100 eggs, sometimes only one baby turtle survives to adulthood.

A loggerhead turtle named Adelita left the west coast of Mexico wearing a device that let scientists track where she went. She swam some 6,000 miles (9,654 km), all the way across the Pacific Ocean, before her signals were lost. She might have been captured by a fishing boat.

These newly hatched loggerhead turtles are scrambling for the ocean in Virginia. When the waves come in, they often push turtle hatchlings farther back up the beach. Then the hatchlings must crawl all the way to the water again, over the same patch of sand they worked so hard to cross the first time.

21

Do Turtles Have Enemies?

Raccoons love to eat turtle eggs, hatchlings, and adults, and they're skilled at finding turtle nests. Unlike many animals, raccoons also do well living near people, where they find plenty of food and have few natural enemies. Some areas with growing numbers of people also have growing numbers of turtle-eating raccoons.

The most dangerous time for a turtle is when it is still in the egg or very young. Many **predators** eat turtle eggs or baby turtles. Raccoons, opossums, skunks, dogs, birds, snakes, and other turtles all eat young freshwater turtles. Sea-turtle eggs and babies are eaten by fish, raccoons, birds, crabs, dogs, and other animals.

If a turtle lives to be an adult, its tough shell and coloring protect it from most enemies. Even so, depending on the species, some turtles are injured or killed by predators. Even huge adult sea turtles are sometimes killed by large predators such as tiger sharks and killer whales.

22

These black vultures and a raccoon-like coati found the nest of an olive ridley turtle in Costa Rica. By the time the photographer took this picture, all of the nest's eggs and hatchlings had been eaten.

This little box turtle is moving as fast as it can across a road in Missouri.

Turtles' worst enemies, however, are people. For thousands of years, people in some parts of the world have eaten turtle meat or eggs or used turtle body parts in medicines. But today, people cause other serious problems for turtles. Thousands of sea turtles every year drown in fishing or shrimping nets, or on long fishing lines that hold thousands of fishhooks. Others die from eating fishing lines and other trash thrown in the water. On land, turtles are hit by cars when they cross roads to get to their nesting areas. Others are taken from their natural surroundings to be sold as pets. An even bigger problem is the loss of areas where the turtles live and nest.

The shells of a sea turtle called the hawksbill turtle have been used to make "tortoiseshell" combs, jewelry, and other items.

Leatherback turtles eat plastic bags floating in the sea, mistaking them for jellyfish.

Fishing nets are a big problem for sea turtles. This green sea turtle got trapped in a fishing net off the coast of Nacaragua. It was trapped near the surface and was able to breathe, but sea turtles that get snagged in deeper nets often drown.

Are Turtles in Danger?

Kemp's ridley turtles nest on only one ocean beach in the world—near Rancho Nuevo, in Mexico.

If a sea turtle runs into trash or is disturbed while she is trying to nest, she might return to the sea without laying her eggs.

Baby sea turtles can't find their way to the ocean if there are bright lights on the beach.

Almost half of the world's turtle species, including all sea turtles, are listed as either threatened or **endangered**. That means they are in danger of dying out. As the number of people grows, ponds and marshes are being turned into farm fields, parking lots, and buildings. Roads, fences, and buildings cut turtles off from their nesting areas. Pollution dirties the water where the turtles live. Scientists are not sure how many species of turtles will be able to survive all these dangers.

Olive ridley turtles like this one are endangered—they nest on only five beaches in the world! Olive ridleys weigh about 100 pounds (45 kg) and have an olive-green, heart-shaped carapace.

Many people are now working to protect turtle species and their homes. In some countries, people who catch shrimp are now using special nets from which turtles can escape. Some sea-turtle nesting sites are protected to keep the eggs and babies from being destroyed. Other wetland and stream areas are being set aside to save the turtles and other animals and plants that live there.

What can we do to help? We can start by learning all we can about these animals and what is happening to them. We can support efforts to save wetlands and other places where turtles live. If we see turtles in the wild, we can leave them where they are instead of disturbing them or keeping them as pets. If we work together, we can make sure that one of nature's most incredible animals will be around for a long, long time.

In some sea-turtle nesting areas, governments are letting local people collect turtle eggs under certain conditions. If the people are allowed to take some eggs, they are sometimes more willing to help protect the rest.

While this Orinoco turtle sunned itself a butterfly landed on its head—and stayed there for a while! These rare turtles live in Venezuela.

29

Glossary

cold-blooded (COLD BLOOD-ed) A cold-blooded animal has a body temperature the same as the temperature around it. Turtles are cold-blooded.

continent (KON-tih-nent) A continent is a huge land area surrounded mostly by water. Of Earth's seven continents, Antarctica is the only one without turtles.

endangered (en-DANE-jerd) An endangered animal is one that is close to dying out. Many types of turtles are endangered.

hibernate (HI-bur-nate) To hibernate is to go into a very deep sleep, to survive through the winter. Some turtles hibernate by burying themselves in the sand or mud.

migrate (MY-grate) To migrate is to travel from one place to another, often to have young. Sea turtles sometimes migrate thousands of miles to lay their eggs.

omnivores (OM-nih-vor) Omnivores are animals that eat both plants and other animals. Many turtles are omnivores.

predators (PRED-uh-terz) Predators are animals that hunt and eat other animals. Raccoons, birds, and even sharks are predators that eat turtles.

reptile (REP-tile) A reptile is an animal that has a backbone, lungs, and a tough skin covered with scales, and that needs outside heat to warm its body. Turtles are reptiles with a shell on the outside.

species (SPEE-sheez) A species is a group of animals that are very much alike and can mate and have babies. There are over 250 species of turtles.

To Find Out More

Read It!

George, William T., and Lindsay Barrett George (illustrator). *Box Turtle at Long Pond.* New York: Greenwillow Books, 1989.

Gibbons, Gail. *Sea Turtles.* New York: Holiday House, 1998.

Guiberson, Brenda Z., and Alix Berenzy (illustrator). *Into the Sea.* New York: Henry Holt, 1996.

Kalman, Bobbie. *The Life Cycle of a Sea Turtle.* New York: Crabtree Publishing, 1997.

Lasky, Kathryn, and Christopher G. Knight (photographer). *Interrupted Journey: Saving Endangered Sea Turtles.* Cambridge, MA: Candlewick Press, 2001.

Trueit, Trudi Strain. *Turtles.* Danbury, CT: Children's Press, 2003.

On the Web

Visit our home page for lots of links about turtles:
http://www.childsworld.com/links

Note to Parents, Teachers, and Librarians: We routinely check our Web links to make sure they're safe, active sites—so encourage your readers to check them out!

Index

About the Author

When Pat Merrick was a child, his family traveled and moved many times. He became fascinated with science and finding out about the world around him. In college he majored in science and education. After college, Mr. Merrick and his wife both decided to become teachers and try and help kids learn to love the world around them. He has taught science to all levels of kids from kindergarten through twelfth grade. When not teaching or writing, Mr. Merrick loves to read and play with his six children. Pat Merrick currently lives in a small town in southern Minnesota with his wife and family.